How to Love Yourself and Your Child

Empowering Parenting Tips

By: Patti Taylor

Table of Contents

Introduction   5

Chapter 1: Motivation, Commitment and Action =   8
Change

Chapter 2: Information and Positive Techniques to   22
Use for Effective Communication, Behavior
Management and Emotional Health

Chapter 3: Self-worth, Self-esteem, and Self-   28
confidence Builders

Chapter 4: Family   34

Chapter 5: Behavior   39

Chapter 6: Positive Steps Towards Well-Being   46

Chapter 7: Self-care for You   48

Chapter 8: Some Additional Thoughts   51

Chapter 9: Some Insights   55

Success Building for Children and Parents

This is a book that offers suggestions on how to empower your child and yourself in a supportive and encouraging way as you move forward to greater understanding of each other.

►Do you have a desire to openly and honestly look at yourself and your child and the relationship that you have?

►Are you willing to change your actions that might not have produced the positive response that you wanted and thereby change your child's response to you?

►What results or changes do you want?

►How can you move forward to achieve positive results?

►How do you create the positive results that you want?

You'll learn some tools and tips that are helpful to you as a parent in building success by working together with your child to create and discover solutions that are empowering and inspiring toward building a successful relationship between your child and yourself.

Introduction

This book presents supportive and encouraging information for anyone that is being challenged with a child demonstrating behavioral or emotional issues. Suggestions are offered with an uplifting and inspiring approach on how to empower your child and yourself as you move forward to greater understanding of each other as you engage with each other in your daily lives.

When I was presented with the behavioral and emotional challenges my child demonstrated in middle school and high school, I sought help and soon became very disappointed with the lack of available information and support regarding services and programs that could benefit my child and help bring me some insight into what was occurring for my child. As I searched for services and programs for my child, I realized that the most important thing I needed was support from understanding people who were either going through what my child and I were going through or had had the experience or knowledge to offer to me. I had to seek out information on my own, and soon I became my child's advocate and that led to being an advocate for change in the community regarding supportive resources for families seeking information on behavioral and emotional issues. Having had first-hand experience, I know how important it is to have information and encouragement presented in a respectful and empowering manner.

Motivation, Commitment and Action = Change

Three very important success-building words:

ENCOURAGE, EMPOWER, and INSPIRE.

A child's behavior is a cry for attention. This is what that behavior is saying: look at me, listen to me, I have a need. Maybe I'm hurting inside, maybe I can't tell you what's wrong, but I'm acting out because that's the only way I can communicate my feelings. I sometimes can't put my feelings in words.

Be Patient. Listen to your child. Practice Active Listening. Your goal is to listen and engage with your child without interrupting so your child knows that you are paying attention to every word he or she is saying.

Talk to you child. Don't yell at your child because he or she will only remember the yelling and the emotion behind it. He or she will just block you and your words out. Keep your cool.

Ask: What's going on? Don't judge your child or the behavior. Find out from your child what happened and why your child re-acted the way that he or she did. Say something like, "I can see that this has upset you."

Routine, structure and limits are what kids love even through they test you on those limits.

Be open to your child; go with your gut feeling with your child.

Move out of the place of feeling you are stuck and nothing is going to change. Set some personal goals for yourself, and then for your child.

Don't bad-mouth yourself in front of your child, your child will pick it up and use it on himself or herself. Remember your child is like a sponge absorbing the positive and the negative.

Try to always come from your heart. Kids can spot phoniness.

You have to invest your heart into your child. Make that connection with him or her by holding both of your child's hands in yours and looking into his or her eyes. Get down to their vision level to make that connection.

Respect your child's thoughts and feelings.

When you trust and respect your child, he or she will trust and respect you.

Develop a personal relationship with your child. Take time to get to know and understand your child. Have everyday conversations with your child; ask your child what he or she did that day, thought about, and would like to talk about.

Set aside a special time and place to be with your child to spend time alone with him or her, just the two of you. Be creative.

Use your imagination, think out-of-the-box when it comes to communicating with your child. Communication cards are a very helpful tool that can be a fun and informative way to engage and connect with your child.

Carve out some family time where the whole family can share their thoughts, ideas and feelings by having a set family day and time.

Let go of the attachment to the outcome, just live in the moment, be there with your child, and don't think about stuff you have to do or should be doing when you are with your child. Focus on your child. Focus on the moment. Be involved in every aspect of your child's life.

Don't bring up stuff that happened in the past, live in the now. Create a new beginning and then proceed to move forward in the adventure of your child's life.

Ask your child: If you could change anything in your life, how would you make it better for yourself?

This is a fresh start, a fresh look at your relationship with your child. You need to get a new perspective on your relationship with your child. Discover your child's personality his likes, dislikes and interests.

You've got to develop a plan that works for you and your child. Children feel safe and secure with structure and routine.

Generate some positive energy by encouraging and empowering your child. Tell him or her that you love him or her. Tell the story of when he or she was born, how much that meant to you, and how much you loved them when they were born and how much you still love them.

Love your child unconditionally. He or she will make mistakes, missteps and misjudgments, but so do we. Together your child and you will learn from these experiences.

In corrective discipline do not use "disappointment." It can be one of the most painful emotions a person could use toward another human being. Do not say, "I am disappointed in you." It is discouraging and negative.

Create a scrapbook or memory book just for your child individually with photos, stories, mementos of their life and your part in it. This will be an on-going project throughout their childhood that each of you can contribute to. This will help you and your child stay focused on the positive aspects of each other and your relationship that will grow and evolve.

Take every opportunity you can to observe and get to know your child. Observe your child: at play, with friends, at school, in the community, at the store, in social settings, etc.

Discover what your child's unique talents and abilities are by observing your child and by simply asking your child what he or she likes to do or would like to do, and then get your child involved and participating in an activity that promotes his or her talent or ability.

Spend some time at your child's school, volunteer for an hour or two a week in the classroom, on the playground, at school activities, after school programs, or field trips. This will strengthen the connection between you and your child and demonstrate to your child that you care and want to be involved in his or her education and activities. Be a willing participant in your child's life.

Think about creating or getting together with other parents and teachers to get a co-op combination online virtual and brick and mortar school started where parents oversee their children and other children taking their online school courses.

Study your child; get to know their triggers, know the signs and re-direct the possible negative behavior into a positive behavior. Give your child a choice of what he or she would like to do that is a positive behavior, because you have most likely experienced this negative behavior before, you can re-direct that negative behavior you see coming into a positive behavior. Your child is challenging and testing your limits of tolerance. Be creative and re-direct the incident or action.

Teach and role model moral values to your child. Your child will be inspired by your positive actions and the example that you set.

Be a role-model for appropriate behavior in all situations – remember your child is watching how you act and react.

Work with your child to develop his or her inspiration or motivation. This could be taking a walk and being inspired by nature, a prayer, a word, a saying, an affirmation, a role model, a positive character in a book or movie, or attending a church service or Sunday school and listening to the message the pastor is giving.

Create an imaginative make-believe or real story with your child in it where he or she is the central character. Have him or her act it out. You could even have your child wear a costume if it suits your story.

Do projects or hobbies together, cook meals together, go fishing, hiking, walking, swimming, exercise together, go bike riding, play a sport together, run together, go to the park, go to museums, go out to eat together, have a picnic, read together, watch an educational or inspirational TV program together, listen to music together, watch a movie together, dance, laugh together, draw with chalk on the sidewalk, blow bubbles, do puzzles together, play together, have a family game night, explore nature together, have a quiet time together, etc.

Every outing, activity, or daily routine can be an opportunity for teaching/training your child social skills, manners, values, and living skills. Make it a fun learning environment.

Get your child to buy into his or her positive behavioral changes by rewarding good behaviors.

Create small goals for your child to achieve, and when he or she has achieved them challenge your child to go further and improve that goal and be even better. All this goal accomplishing is leading to your child becoming successful in life, and moving toward becoming a responsible individual with your guidance and love.

When a negative behavior occurs ask your child what he or she would have done differently.

Come from the heart. Show love and nurturing to your child. Tell him or her everyday that you love him or her.

Love your child. Let your child know that you care about him or her, and that what he or she is thinking and experiencing is important to you.

Encourage your child by creating an atmosphere that will allow your child to express who he or she is in a positive way.

Challenge your child to work toward positive behaviors.

Change the negative action, word or feeling using a positive response.

Be positive. Praise and reward your child. A reward doesn't have to cost money. It can be your child spending time alone with you doing something you both enjoy.

See your child objectively. Get to know all the aspects of your child and work with their positive traits and build upon those.

Your child's behavior will change slowly by small steps. Don't give up – celebrate the small steps.

Is everyday a challenge and a victory? Yes!

Encourage your child to express his or her needs and desires.

Assist your child in expressing his or her feelings by using feelings words: *I feel, I need*. Communication is essential.

Help develop your child's emotional intelligence: their self-awareness, self-management, social awareness and relationship management.

Never give up. Don't expect behaviors to change overnight. It is a process. It takes time to change a behavior. Be consistent, the results will come.

The Whole Person: Using these tools and strategies will help in facilitating the development of your child in becoming whole and to accept his or her wholeness. These tools and strategies will work for us too.

With continued practice and consistency you will see the positive effects and results that you desire.

Strong, confident, competent and knowledgeable families that are able to be deeply involved with their children's lives and upbringing are the greatest contributors to their children's progress and well being.

emotion

face feeling expressing sense creative expression people attention indicate mood nerve

Information and Positive Techniques to Use for Effective Communication, Behavior Management and Emotional Health

Indentify Feelings

USE statements like these:

I Feel statements: *I feel frustrated.*

I need statements: *I need to be listened to, I need to have a voice.*

These statements help individuals to identify feelings and also identify separately what it is that he or she needs in order to cope with or solve a problem.

Identifying needs is prerequisite for expressing wants or needs.

Focus on "I statements" – to teach expression of wants and needs, not "You statements" that blame other people and put the responsibility outside of you.

"I statements" takes ownership: I feel, I believe, I think.

EXAMPLE: *I feel sad when it rains because I want to go outside and play with my friends.*

Talk Blocks can help individuals to identify feelings, and also identify separately what it is that he or she needs in order to cope with or solve a problem.

Children's Feelings Words

Happy Words
Calm

Peaceful

Joyful

Cheerful

Safe

Sad Words
Disappointed

Discouraged

Miserable

Hurt

Depressed

Mad Words
Annoyed

Crabby

Grouchy

Furious

Frustrated

Afraid Words
Anxious

Frightened

Nervous

Scared

Worried

Are There Things I Can Control?

Things I can control:

My words
My actions
My ideas
My play
My mistakes

Things out of my control:

Others' words
Actions of others
My friends' ideas
Others' play
Others' mistakes

Coping/Calming Skills

I can calm myself by:

Taking 3 deep breaths
Count from 1 to 10
Talk to an adult or friend about what is bothering you
Get a hug or give a hug
Draw a picture of why you're angry
Jump up and down for a minute
Listen to music
Sing a song
Hit a pillow
Tense and relax your muscles
Talk yourself into being calm: say, "Be calm, be calm or I can handle this."
Exercise: ride a bike, take a walk

learning personality stress life coach develop valuable connection cultural

communicate work inner skills goals

effective behavior cultivate interpersonal manage

PEOPLE SKILLS

help extrovert important success social skill set

ability people self interactions

business acquire self awareness introvert

develop emotional alliances

Emotional intelligence – What is it?

It is self-awareness: The capability to recognize your own emotions and how these emotions affect your thoughts and behavior, how to know your own strengths and weaknesses, and have self-confidence.

It is self-management: The capability to control your impulsive feelings and behaviors, to manage your emotions in an appropriate healthy manner, to be able to take initiative, to be able to follow through on commitments, and to be able to adapt to changing circumstances in your life.

It is social awareness: The capability to understand the emotions, needs and concerns of other people, understand emotional cues, feel at ease socially, and recognize the unseen and unspoken power dynamics in a group or organization.

It is relationship management: The capability to develop and maintain good relationships with others, to express yourself clearly, inspire and influence others, work well in a team environment, and to be able to manage conflict.

Self-worth, Self-esteem, and Self-confidence Builders

Positive Affirmations

Affirm your positive statements – *I am wonderful, I am creative, I am positive, I am … My child is ….* Own your beliefs and values.

Use positive statements with your child – *I am so proud of you, you are a star, what a great job you did, you are so smart, that took a lot of courage, etc.*

Self-talk

Before a situation occurs:
Take a few deep breaths beforehand.
Plan how to deal with the situation.
No matter what happens, you are still a good person.

During the situation:
Stay cool. Be in control.
Stick to the current issue.
You have a right to your opinion and your point of view.

Cope – Use self-talk if you feel overwhelmed or if the situation is getting out of hand:
Take a moment to breathe.
Don't get angry or let the person rattle you.
You can say that you want to address the situation after a break.
Give yourself time to re-group your thoughts.

After the situation has occurred:
Evaluate how you handled the situation.
If resolved: Congratulate yourself. Be proud of yourself.
If unresolved: You can do it better or differently next time.

Teach and Role-Model Moral Values

Kindheartedness: compassionate

Self-reliance: responsible

Humility: admitting one's mistake

Mutual respect: respect for others

Love: for life, country, peace and harmony

Justice: just and fair

Freedom: of choice

Courage: brave

Cleanliness of body and mind: physical cleanliness, healthy thoughts

Honesty/integrity: sincere

Diligence: determined

Cooperation: helping one another

Moderation: not excessive in words or actions

Gratitude: thankful

Rationality: able to reason

Public spiritedness: aware of social issues in the community

Create A Family Vision

A family vision is a short statement created and owned by the family. Develop your own family vision.

If you were able to change certain things in your family's life for the better, what would you change to make things better?

Create your (parents) vision:

Have your child create his or her vision:

Now combine the two visions into one statement making it your family's vision.

Participate in A Talking Circle

Sit down in a circle with your child or children and pass an object like a talking stick to one person while everyone else is quiet and listening to the person talking. Have that person talk about something like these topics or make up one: Animals, Planets, Oceans, Action heroes, a Princess, a Prince, Flowers, Trees, Feelings, When I grow up I want to be…, What makes you feel safe? Anything you want to talk about.

Family

Examples of Conversation Topics to Use for Communication

1. Who is someone you look up to and why?

2. What do you worry about?

3. What is your most embarrassing moment?

4. What is your favorite food?

5. Talk about a time you felt really proud?

6. How are you a good friend?

7. What's your favorite sport?

8. Talk about a time you felt really angry?

9. What would you like to change about the world?

10. Talk about a time you felt really sad?

11. What's your favorite holiday?

12. What' your favorite movie?

13. What are 3 things you do well?

14. What's the craziest thing you've ever done?

Have Family Meetings

Weekly family meetings are an effective and informal way to bring the family together, to improve communication, to set weekly goals, to recognize and reward progress, and to discuss each member's needs and feelings.

1. The meetings should be set at a regular, pleasant time—for instance, after dinner, with dessert.

2. Parents can be facilitators as discussion leaders and can make sure that any ground rules are clearly explained and understood.

3. The meetings should emphasize both individual and family needs, goals and accomplishments and discuss positive events and efforts. During the meeting parents might give allowances and praise and reward behavior progress and changes. They can also share other upcoming events or important family information, such as an upcoming family vacation, holiday plans or school event to prepare for.

4. Each family member should be allowed to speak freely without criticism or interruption, to share his or her thoughts, feelings, achievements, and hopes.

5. Family meetings should be upbeat and encouraging. The meeting is not a time or place to scold, punish, recall past mistakes, blow off steam, or single out a

particular person. Those issues should be taken up separately and individually.

6. The meetings should last no more than twenty or thirty minutes unless the family wants to continue.

7. When discussing difficult issues, everyone in the family should understand and accept that parents have the final word in difficult decisions.

8. A record should be kept of the main points, rewards, progress toward goals, new goals, and agreements and/or changes.

9. Before the meeting ends, anyone who wants to should have a chance to say how he or she thinks the meeting went, and what improvements might be done to make the next meeting better.

Hints

Do you or your child like to: write creatively, tell creative stories, dance, sing, play music, draw or paint, read, participate in sports, exercise, create crafts or play video games?

Believe it or not by asking these things it tells you what kind of communication and learning style you or your child has. For example: a child that likes to read is a child that is a visual learner.

Provide positive outlets for your child like physical activities and creative outlets.

Age appropriate activities are essential. It's important to offer your child a physical outlet. Participating in sports or a physical activity of some kind that your child likes is a good outlet for excess energy. Creative outlets such as art, music, acting, and writing will allow your child to express his or herself in a constructive way. Journaling is a beneficial outlet for your child and yourself.

Behavior Management Tips

Role Modeling – is modeling the positive behavior or behaviors you want your child to do or have. Remember children do what is modeled in front of them whether it is positive or negative. Children learn behaviors by what they see, not by what they are told.

Re-directing – Redirecting a child by changing the activity may be enough of a change for a child to calm down and return to a normal functioning level. This method of distracting a child's energy or attention to a substitute activity can de-escalate the situation and help the child maintain control.

Cueing – Sometimes a child's attention to a potentially disruptive stimulus can be interrupted with cues (usually non-verbal) such as raised eyebrows, eye contact or clearing the throat. This technique is most effective prior to a child engaging in misbehavior.

Prompting – involves signaling either verbally or non-verbally to a child to either begin a desired behavior or to stop an undesired behavior. Prompting can be a simple direction given when a child needs help in progressing or transitioning to the next step.

Active listening – Sometimes, instead of attempting to understand a child's feelings, we may make statements that discourage children for expressing their feelings. Active listening is a means to allow and encourage the communication of needs and to validate feelings indicating interest, understanding and acceptance. It is best used as an early intervention technique to encourage children to "talk out" rather than "act out".

Change the Environment – This may be used when a child's behavior has reached a point where it is best to ask him or her to leave the immediate environment for a few minutes. This technique is used merely to give the child an opportunity to regroup and regain control and is not to be confused with time out. A child may be asked to get a drink of water or to wash up for dinner, or may be directed to take a walk with the adult.

Problem solving – is breaking down a problem that is overwhelming and solving it through small manageable steps. The basic steps are: the process of recognizing a problem, defining it, identifying alternative plans to resolve the problem, selecting a plan, organizing steps of the plan, implementing the plan, and evaluating the outcome.

Challenging Behavior Explanation

Children will engage in challenging behavior because it "works" for them.

When a child uses challenging behavior it results in the child gaining or obtaining access to something or avoiding something

Some challenging behaviors are just a part of normal development of communication and self-regulation.

Why Does Challenging Behavior Happen?

It serves a purpose or function for the child.
It is often a form of communication.

Children can communicate their behavior in many ways

Forms of communication could be:

Words
Sentences
Eye stare or facial expression
Body language: using hands, fists or arms
Biting, hitting, kicking, or pinching
Tantrums: screaming, yelling

Children communicate using a variety of messages or meanings

Some functions of communication could be

To ask for an object, activity or person that they want

To escape demands placed upon them

To escape an activity that they don't want to do

It could be a request for help

It may be a desire for social interaction

To get a reaction or attention from the adult/parent

It could be a form of asking for information

However it is typically to obtain something or to get away from something or someone

Prevention

In adult (parent)-child interactions – be sure to give positive attention

Have an organized environment with structure, routine and a schedule

Put in to practice social skills and behavioral rules and expectations

Prevention Strategies

Identify and remove the "trigger" (something that sets off the behavior) that is the cause of challenging behaviors.

Remove, modify or change the environment to prevent the behavior, making it more agreeable to the child.

Use replacement skills (techniques that will replace the negative behavior with a positive behavior) – Teach and reinforce these skills in the morning, after school and at bedtime.

Use solutions that are workable for your child, you and others

A specific intervention (behavior management technique) is corresponded to the reason for the behavior.

Intervention techniques are hands-on

The focus is on teaching new skills to re-direct, modify or change the behavior.

Create a Chore and Reward/Consequence Jar

Takes the guess work out of coming up with a chore or a reward or consequence. Involves all family members. Reduces stress and encourages the child to take responsibility for his or her actions.

Positive Steps Towards Wellbeing

Be kind to yourself: Encourage yourself rather that criticize yourself.

Take up a hobby or learn a new skill: It will increase your confidence in yourself.

Help others: You will feel better about yourself.

Eat healthily: Your body will feel better.

Connect with others: Stay in contact with family and friends.

See the bigger picture: Broaden your perspective.

Exercise regularly: Benefits our health, reduces stress, gives us more energy.

Be creative: Increases our self-confidence.

Relax: Breathe. Make time for yourself.

Develop a healthy sleep routine.

Balance: Your work, family time and social activities.

Self-care for You

Be good to yourself-love yourself. Take time for yourself. Physically: exercise, get a massage, eat healthy foods, drink lots of water, and rest.

Spiritually, emotionally, and mentally: read a book, meditate, pray, dream, plan, expand your world with art, music, good friends and conversation.

What's your inspiration? Maybe it's cooking, writing, walking, meditating, being in nature, music, surrounding yourself with positive people, religious or spiritual practices, motivational speakers, reading a self-help book, saying positive affirmations, singing, playing an instrument, being in a loving relationship, feeling loved, etc.

LOVE your self

Take Time for Yourself - _Love yourself._

Why? I thought that was selfish and that I'm supposed to put others' needs before me. That's what I absorbed from my parents, relatives, church, teachers, and others throughout the years. I'd feel guilty, egotistical, self-absorbed if I was to love myself. As a mother and former wife I gave love, but couldn't allow myself to be loved because I didn't love me. I could always find some flaw in me to dislike. And the longer I could continue to dislike and not love myself; I could stay in my comfort zone. I could be miserable and attract others to me who didn't love themselves either. Now I want to break this cycle. I am a beautiful creature with a beautiful soul and loving heart that has accepted that it is good to love and nurture myself. That it's ok to love the person I was in the past, the person I am now and the person I am becoming because each of us is a reflection of God and who is God but love. So why shouldn't I love me. God loves me and now I give myself permission to love myself.

How can I feel and show that I love me today? I can spend time with myself and be a friend to myself. I will respect myself. I will respect my thoughts, my feelings and my body. I will be open to my soul, my dreams, my visions, and my goals and not condemn myself for any thought or feeling. I will love myself unconditionally. By changing this pattern in my life I can affect change in my children, my family, my friends and the people I interact with daily in all situations. I will feel positive about myself and love myself and thereby be able to help others because I am helping me love me. I find when I love myself I feel better physically, mentally, spiritually and emotionally.

Take time for yourself, love yourself and be good to yourself. Start nurturing yourself first, then your child. You are important to yourself and to your child.

Some additional thoughts

Dream with your child. Show your child kindness. Increase your child's self-esteem. Inspire your child. By doing this you will propel your child forward. Find at least one thing a day that your child did that is positive and praise your child to boost his or her self-esteem, self-worth and self-confidence, even if your child challenged you with his or her behavior that day. Be confident; don't be discouraged. One technique or solution may work for a while or this time, but might not work the next. *Be creative. Be inventive.* Explore what works for your child.

Your child is always evolving and moving forward on his or her path. Be flexible. Negotiate with your child; give your child choices, offer options. Change the negative situation into a positive one. Work toward a win-win solution for both of you.

Create a Positive Statement

I will work toward achieving results with…

(you provide the answer).

Your answer could be: *with the support of others.*

Write down the positive qualities your child has and build upon them.

<u>Journal</u>

This is a form of releasing and communication; this is where you let it out, talk to yourself through your words, write your own story. Add to this the discoveries that you have made and are making about yourself, your life, your path, your child, your family, your goals, your dreams, your passions, and your future.

Love

Some Insights

Love - *The powerful meaning of this word when applied to a mother and her child. (Substitute father, family member or whatever special relationship you have with this child.)*

The love a mother has for her child. This kind of love that a mother feels toward her child is such a strong emotion that written or spoken words can't convey the power of this word. Love has to be felt by the giver and receiver. It comes from the heart. What makes this kind of love so special is that it is pure, honest, and doesn't have any strings attached. It is unconditional love. There is no obstacle too great for a mother to hurdle to get or give help to her child. When her child is faced with a challenge, a mother will activate her natural warrior like ability that gives her strength to seek victory. This challenge becomes her cause and her passion. Is everyday a challenge and a victory? Yes!

Patti Taylor

Patti has Family Support Partner and Life Coaching certificates and numerous parenting and behavioral management trainings. She has worked with parents instructing them in parenting skills and behavioral management techniques. She has worked with children instructing them in social skills and behavior management, using social stories, re-direction and role-modeling techniques. She is a single mom and has appeared on Channel 8 AZ Horizon's show describing some of the challenges she faced as she sought information, help and support for her child and herself.